MW00396276

 Essential Question
What jobs need to be done in a community?

At Work with Mom

by Arlene Block

illustrated by Jason Wolff

CHAPTER 1

A Big Day

It is a big day. Jen goes to work with her mom.

Jen's mom is a doctor. Dr. Deb helps kids. She helps them when they are sick. She helps them stay healthy.

Brand X Pictures/Punchstock

"Here we are," says Mom.

"Cool," says Jen. "I can't wait to see your new office!"

Brand X Pictures/Punchstock

Jen and Mom step inside. Jen sees a room where people wait. No one is there yet.

Brand X Pictures/Punchstock

4

Miss Rex sits here. She helps Mom. She answers the phone and greets people when they come in.

"Good morning," says Miss Rex. "It will be a busy day. Lots of kids are coming in for check ups."

Brand X Pictures/Punchstock

CHAPTER 3

The Exam Rooms

Mom and Jen go to an exam room.
Ed is getting the room ready.
Ed is a nurse.

"Ed checks the kids before I see them," says Mom. "Then I do the rest of the exam."

Brand X Pictures/Punchstock

"Let me show you what I do," says Ed. "First, I check to see how much you have grown."

"Next, I check your heartbeat," he says. "Then I check to see that your heart is strong."

Later, Ed takes Jen to meet Meg.

"What is that?" asks Jen, pointing to a big machine.

"It's an X-ray machine," says Meg. "I use it to take pictures. The pictures show the inside of your body."

8

Brand X Pictures/Punchstock

Meg shows Jen a picture.

"This picture shows a broken leg," says Meg. "It shows where the bone has to be fixed."

Jen looks at more pictures. Then she heads back to see Miss Rex.

CHAPTER 4

A Big Mess

"Oh, no!" yells Jen. "What a mess!"

Jen looks around and sees some empty bins. She has an idea.

"I can help you, Miss Rex," Jen says. "I can use these bins."

Brand X Pictures/Punchstock

Jen gets to work. Soon there is no more mess.

"Thank you for your help, Jen," says Miss Rex. "I hope you come to work with your mom again!"

Brand X Pictures/Punchstock

Respond to Reading

Retell

Use your own words to retell events in *At Work with Mom*.

Character	Setting	Events

Text Evidence

1. Who is Dr. Deb and where does she work? Character, Setting, Events

2. Who works in Dr. Deb's office? What do they do?
Character, Setting, Events

3. How can you tell that *At Work with Mom* is realistic fiction? Genre

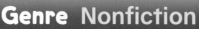

Compare Texts
How is a school nurse like
a doctor?

Steve Hix/Somos Images/Corbis

Tools
for the
School
Nurse

A school nurse helps you when you are sick or get hurt. What tools does a school nurse use?

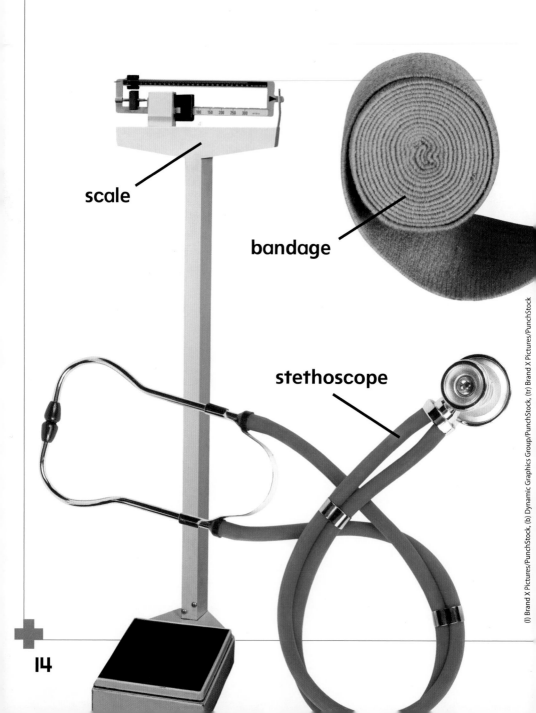

scale

bandage

stethoscope

(l) Brand X Pictures/PunchStock, (b) Dynamic Graphics Group/PunchStock, (tr) Brand X Pictures/PunchStock

thermometer

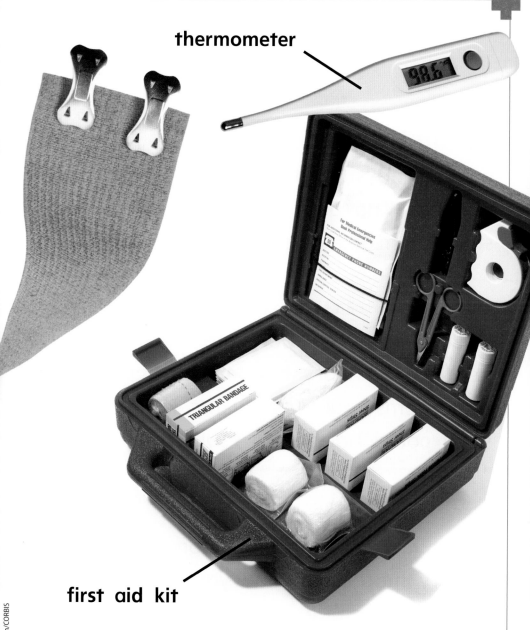

first aid kit

(tr) D. Hurst/Alamy, (b) Lew Robertson/CORBIS

Make Connections

How is a school nurse like the nurse in *At Work with Mom*? Text to Text

Focus on Genre

Realistic Fiction Realistic fiction is a made-up story that could happen in real life. The people and places in the story seem like real people and places.

What to Look for The characters in *At Work with Mom* are like real people. The story happens in a place that seems real. The events in the story could happen in real life.

Your Turn

Plan a realistic fiction story. Make a story map to outline your story. Be sure to include characters, settings, and events that could be real. Tell what happens in the beginning, in the middle, and at the end of the story.